Court Is in Session

FEDERAL COURTS

JENNA TOLLI

PowerKiDS press™

NEW YORK

Published in 2020 by The Rosen Publishing Group, Inc.
29 East 21st Street, New York, NY 10010

Editor: Jane Katirgis
Book Design: Rachel Rising

Photo Credits: Cover Photo by Mike Kline (notkalvin)/Moment/Getty Images; Cover, pp. 1, 3, 4, 5, 6, 7, 8, 9, 10, 11, 12, 13, 14, 15, 16, 17, 18, 19, 20, 21, 22, 23, 24, 25, 26, 27, 28, 29, 30, 31, 32 (background) Allgusak/Shutterstock.com; pp. 4, 6, 8, 12, 20, 26 (gavel) AVA Bitter/Shutterstock.com; p. 5 artboySHF/Shutterstock.com; p. 7 Palau/Shutterstock.com; pp. 9, 27 Bettman/Contributor/Getty Images; p. 10 STAN HONDA/AFP/Getty Images; p. 11 Mark Van Scyoc/Shutterstock.com; p. 13 https://commons.wikimedia.org/wiki/File:US_Court_of_Appeals_and_District_Court_map.svg; pp. 15, 23 sirtravelalot/Shutterstock.com; p. 17 Donaldson Collection/Micheal Ochs Archives/Getty Images; p. 19 Rob Crandall/Shutterstock.com; p. 21 cabania/Shutterstock.com; p. 22 Mario Villafuerte/Stringer/Getty Images New/Getty Images; p. 25 Allkindza/iStock Unreleased/Getty Images; p. 29 ImageCatcher News Service/Corbis Historical/Getty Images; p. 30 Onur ERSIN/Shutterstock.com.

Library of Congress Cataloging-in-Publication Data

Names: Tolli, Jenna, author.
Title: Federal courts / Jenna Tolli.
Description: New York : PowerKids Press, [2020] | Series: Court is in session
   | Includes index.
Identifiers: LCCN 2018020443| ISBN 9781538343227 (library bound) | ISBN
   9781538343203 (pbk.) | ISBN 9781538343210 (6 pack)
Subjects: LCSH: Courts--United States--Juvenile literature. | Justice,
   Administration of--United States--Juvenile literature.
Classification: LCC KF8720 .T65 2019 | DDC 347.73/2--dc23
LC record available at https://lccn.loc.gov/2018020443

Manufactured in the United States of America

CPSIA Compliance Information: Batch #CSPK19 For further information contact Rosen Publishing, New York, New York at 1-800-237-9932.

Contents

HISTORY OF FEDERAL COURTS

The United States Constitution went into effect in 1789. It created laws that govern the country, and it provides rights to American citizens. Although the Constitution doesn't explain how to set up the different types of federal courts, it does provide a starting point. Article III of the Constitution states there will be one U.S. Supreme Court. It also gives Congress the ability to create inferior, or lower level, courts when they're needed. This is how our federal court system was created.

Not All Cases Are Federal

Federal courts only hear certain types of cases. If the issue in question may **violate** the Constitution or a federal law, it's handled in federal court. This is called "federal question jurisdiction." Federal courts also hear cases between two parties when those parties aren't from the same state or country. This is called "diversity of citizenship," which helps prevent unfair advantages to one side based on their location.

It's important that we have different levels of federal courts to make sure our justice system is balanced.

Congress first decided how the federal courts would be organized in the Judiciary Act of 1789. "Judiciary" refers to things that have to do with courts of law. This act created the different levels of federal courts that we have today.

DIFFERENT LEVELS

There are three main levels of federal courts in our country: district courts, the U.S. courts of appeals, and the Supreme Court. There are also other federal courts that only handle specific topics.

Each type of court serves an important purpose in the legal system. District courts are at the bottom level. These are where trials are held for the first time. The middle level has the courts of appeals. An appeal is when someone who lost a case makes a formal request to reverse a **verdict**. These courts have the power

Hazelwood v. Kuhlmeier

In the important case *Hazelwood v. Kuhlmeier* (1988), student **journalists** felt their freedom of speech rights were violated when the school principal removed certain articles from their school newspaper. The district court sided with the school and ruled that student rights weren't violated. The students appealed to the U.S. Court of Appeals for the Eighth Circuit, which reversed the decision. The school appealed to the Supreme Court, which made the final decision that students' rights hadn't been violated.

THREE LEVELS OF FEDERAL COURTS

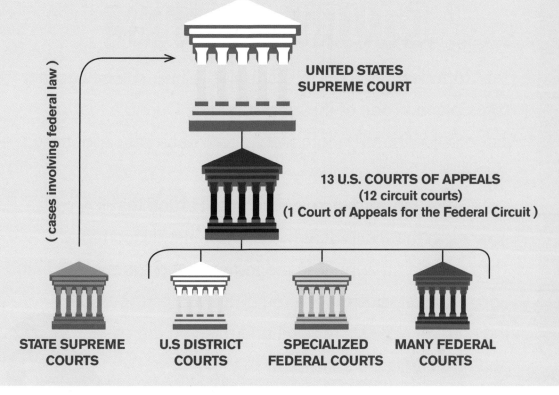

(cases involving federal law)

UNITED STATES SUPREME COURT

13 U.S. COURTS OF APPEALS
(12 circuit courts)
(1 Court of Appeals for the Federal Circuit)

STATE SUPREME COURTS

U.S DISTRICT COURTS

SPECIALIZED FEDERAL COURTS

MANY FEDERAL COURTS

When someone asks a higher court to review the decision of a lower court with the hope that it'll change the result, this is called an appeal. The courts of appeals and the Supreme Court hear appeals. The power to hear an appeal is called "appellate jurisdiction."

to review and change a verdict that's already been made by a district court. The highest level of federal court is the U.S. Supreme Court, where decisions made by any lower court could be **overturned** or **upheld**.

CLIMBING THE COURT SYSTEM

A federal court case starts with a trial. The trial usually takes place in one of the district courts. During a trial, a judge or jury considers the facts from each side and makes a verdict.

After the verdict, one side might argue that there was an error in the trial or that the law was used incorrectly. They can file an appeal. In the federal court system, the first appeal usually goes to the region's court of appeals. If the court of appeals reviews and rules on the case and one party isn't satisfied with the new verdict,

Brown v. Board of Education

One example of a landmark case is *Brown v. Board of Education* (1954), which had to do with racial segregation in public schools. The U.S. District Court for the District of Kansas originally heard the case, but the Supreme Court made the final ruling. The Supreme Court ruled it was unconstitutional to separate races in public schools.

LANDMARK CASES

When the decision from a federal court case shapes our country's history and impacts citizens throughout the nation, it's called a "landmark case."

The power of a court to hear a trial for the first time is called "original jurisdiction." District courts have original jurisdiction, but the U.S. courts of appeals don't because they only hear appeals of existing cases. The Supreme Court usually handles appeals, but it also hears trials in rare cases.

The News

HIGH COURT BANS SEGREGATION IN PUBLIC SCHOOLS

the party could appeal to the Supreme Court. However, the Supreme Court gets to decide which cases it'll review, and it doesn't accept many cases. This means it's rare for the Supreme Court to hear a case and overturn a verdict.

DISTRICT COURTS

District courts are where federal trials take place. During a trial, facts and **evidence** are presented to a judge and jury. Juries are made up of citizens and are meant to give **impartial** opinions on the case. The judge or the jury decides whether someone is guilty or innocent based on the evidence presented in court.

States with multiple districts are split up by geographic area. For example, New York has four court districts: Northern, Southern, Eastern, and Western. The United States District Court for the Eastern District of New York is shown here.

UNITED STATES COURTHOUSE

There are 94 district courts. There's at least one district in each U.S. state and in U.S. territories such as Puerto Rico. Some states with higher populations have up to four federal court districts. Each district also has a **bankruptcy** court, which is a separate unit of the district court system.

U.S. COURTS OF APPEALS

The U.S. courts of appeals decide whether laws were correctly applied in federal court trials. After a district court hears the case, the losing side may request an appeal. The first level of this process usually goes to the regional court of appeals.

There are 13 courts that make up the federal courts of appeals. They're also called circuit courts. The 94 district courts are organized into 12 numbered geographic regions made up of U.S. states or territories, including the District of Columbia.

Evarts Act

The Judiciary Act of 1891, known as the Evarts Act, created the structure of the U.S. courts of appeals. This act created circuit courts to handle most appeals from the lower courts. This was meant to reduce the number of cases the Supreme Court had to review.

The number of states covered by one circuit court depends on the population. This is why some circuits have only a few states but others have more.

GEOGRAPHIC BOUNDARIES
of United States Courts of Appeals and United States District Courts

Each of these circuits hears appeals from a certain area of the country. There's also a Court of Appeals for the Federal Circuit, which hears special cases from across the country regardless of the region.

13

USUALLY THE
FINAL DECISION

The U.S. courts of appeals have the final decision in thousands of federal court cases every year. Certain cases could also move on to be reviewed by the Supreme Court after one of the circuit courts makes a decision. However, the Supreme Court accepts very few cases per year. This means for most appeals cases, the court of appeals will be the last stage of review.

One example of a case where the final decision was made by a court of appeals is *Glik v. Cunniffe* (2011). In this case, the United States Court of Appeals for the First Circuit ruled that police and public officials can be filmed in public places by private citizens, within reason.

FILING AN APPEAL

There should be a legal reason to file an appeal besides disagreement with the verdict. If someone feels there was an error in their trial, they can file an appeal.

When a party appeals its case, that party's lawyer will need to explain to the group of judges or justices why they believe an error was made in the original case.

U.S. SUPREME COURT

The Supreme Court is the highest level in the federal court system and the only court established in the Constitution. The biggest role, or part, of this court is to review the decisions made by lower appeals courts and decide whether to uphold that verdict. The Supreme Court also has original jurisdiction; it has the power to hear trials for the first time, too. This power is used when one state files a case against another or for cases between states and the United States, but this doesn't happen as often.

The Supreme Court receives more than 7,000 requests per year to review cases from other courts. It will choose only 80 to 150 of those requests to review.

THE TITLE OF JUSTICE

Members of the Supreme Court are referred to as "justices" rather than "judges." When a justice is appointed to the court, they serve until they retire, die, or are **impeached**.

The Constitution doesn't state how many justices should serve on the Supreme Court at once. The number has changed over time, but it's nine as of 2018.

TO THE TOP

Some reasons that a case goes to the Supreme Court are if the lower courts had different opinions, if the case is related to the U.S. Constitution or federal laws, or if the case has national **significance**.

When the Supreme Court hears a case, justices will first read a brief, or review, that explains the legal details of the case. Next, the justices hear arguments from lawyers on each side of the case and can ask the lawyers questions. The justices meet together to discuss the case and make their decisions. When more than half of the justices agree to the outcome, that's the majority opinion. The court's final decision and its explanation for the decision are then released to the public.

WRIT OF CERTIORARI

When the Supreme Court decides to hear a case, it issues a "writ of certiorari." This is how higher courts request **documents** from lower courts to review a case.

The Supreme Court building in Washington, D.C., is open to the public. Visitors can explore parts of the historical building and even attend court sessions.

OTHER COURTS

There are other federal trial courts in our justice system that just handle cases about specific subjects. For example, the United States Court of International Trade only hears cases about international trade laws and customs laws. This includes cases that involve laws and taxes on **imported** goods.

The United States Court of Federal Claims hears cases regarding financial claims against the federal government. This court hears cases that have to do with taxes, private property taken by the government for public use, contract disagreements, and many other topics.

Federal Appeals Courts

There are other federal courts created by Congress that handle specific types of appeals. The U.S. Court of Appeals for Veterans Claims hears disputes regarding veterans' benefits and programs. The U.S. Court of Appeals for the Armed Forces handles cases for active military members and anyone who is subject to military laws. This court might hear cases about the rights of service members.

The U.S. Tax Court does not use juries to decide cases. Instead, cases in this court are presented to a single judge.

The U.S. Tax Court handles cases related to taxpayer **disputes**. This might include disagreements about federal income tax or interest claims between citizens and the federal government.

CRIMINAL RIGHTS

Decisions made in federal courts have changed the way our country handles criminal rights. For example, the ruling of *Miranda v. Arizona* in 1966 changed how **suspects** are informed of their rights during arrest. In this case, the Supreme Court ruled that police and law enforcement officials must inform suspects about their right to have a lawyer represent them and the right against self-incrimination. Self-incrimination is when someone provides information that can be used against them in court. Police now recite these rights to suspects. This is called a Miranda warning.

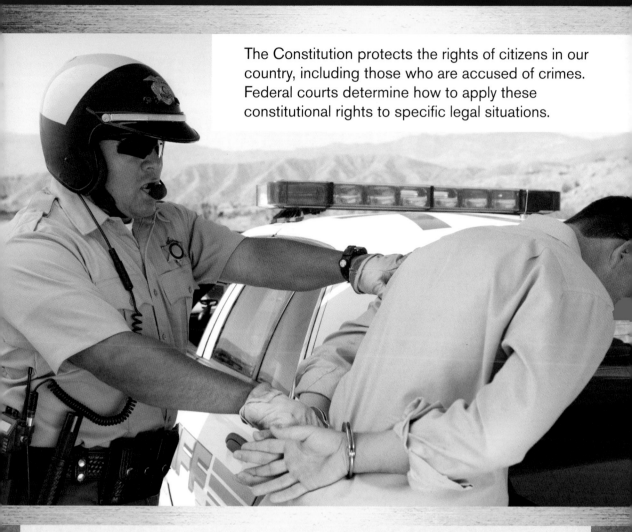

The Constitution protects the rights of citizens in our country, including those who are accused of crimes. Federal courts determine how to apply these constitutional rights to specific legal situations.

In the case *Mapp v. Ohio* (1961), the Supreme Court ruled that police officers must show a search warrant to search someone's house. If evidence is **obtained** illegally, it can't be used in court. This is important to our Fourth Amendment rights, which protect against unreasonable searches.

DECISIONS THAT AFFECT EVERYONE

We know the decisions made in federal courts affect the people who are on trial, but they can also affect the whole country. During the presidential election in 2000, the total number of votes in Florida for George W. Bush and Al Gore was very close. A case was filed (*Bush v. Gore*) to decide whether there should be a recount of votes in certain areas. The U.S. Supreme Court ruled that it would violate the Constitution to finish the recount, since it was done differently throughout the state.

In another case, *National Federation of Independent Business v. Sebelius* (2012), the Supreme Court upheld most of the Affordable Care Act. The Affordable Care Act determined the way many American citizens would receive health insurance and changed the way our country's health-care system works.

Not all federal court cases affect our country as a whole, but when a case has high national importance, the Supreme Court often handles it.

RIGHTS FOR STUDENTS

Decisions made in federal courts affect students' rights in schools, too. When a student or a student's family feels their constitutional rights have been violated, they may file a federal court case.

A landmark case for the right to free speech in schools is *Tinker v. Des Moines* (1969). In Des Moines, Iowa, students wore armbands to school to protest the Vietnam War and were suspended when they refused to remove them. Parents of these students filed a case against the school. After a U.S. district court and a U.S. court of appeals let the suspension stand,

Engel v. Vitale

Another important case for rights in schools is *Engel v. Vitale* (1962). Students were asked to recite a prayer in school every morning in New York public schools. Some families filed a court case because they believed school-sponsored prayer was unconstitutional. In this case, the Supreme Court ruled that the formal prayers violated the First Amendment clause separating the government from religion.

STUDENTS' RIGHTS

Federal courts also hear cases about fair treatment during the judicial process. In the case *Goss v. Lopez* (1975), the Supreme Court ruled that students have the right to a hearing before being suspended from school.

A student or a student's family could file a court case if they feel their rights have been violated in school. In this picture, Mary Beth and John Tinker from the *Tinker v. Des Moines* case show the armbands that started the case.

the Supreme Court ultimately ruled that students have the right to free speech in school and that the armbands didn't disturb learning.

THE FUTURE OF FEDERAL COURTS

When a federal judge or justice leaves their position due to retirement, death, or impeachment, a new justice must take the position. The U.S. president nominates federal court judges and justices when there's an opening. The president usually nominates a candidate who shares his political views. Since judges serve longer than presidents do, this is a way to continue political influence after the president leaves office. After the president nominates someone to be a judge on a federal court, the Senate Judiciary Committee interviews the candidate to decide whether they're right for the position.

Since federal judges and justices typically serve life terms, the president can only make appointments when there's an opening. This means the federal judges and justices that serve today have been appointed by several different presidents.

Elena Kagan was nominated for the Supreme Court by President Obama. Her appointment was confirmed after the Senate Judiciary Committee hearing.

CONTINUING CHANGE

The federal justice system in the United States has changed over time. When the Constitution was drafted over 200 years ago, the Founding Fathers knew that new courts might need to be created to serve the changing legal needs of our country. They gave Congress the power to create inferior courts in Article III of the Constitution for this reason.

It might seem like verdicts made in federal courts only affect the people involved in the case, but we can see that these decisions have also impacted our society as a whole. From freedom of speech in schools to health-care laws, the important decisions made in federal courts continue to affect the lives of citizens in our country.

GLOSSARY

bankruptcy: The state of not having enough money to pay what you owe.

dispute: A disagreement or argument.

document: A formal piece of writing.

evidence: Something that shows that something else is true.

impartial: Fair, without taking sides.

impeach: To charge a public official with a crime done in office.

import: To bring into a country from another.

journalist: Someone who works with the collecting, writing, and editing of news stories for newspapers, magazines, websites, television, or radio.

obtain: To get or receive.

overturn: Reverse.

significance: Influence, importance.

suspect: A person who is believed to be possibly guilty of committing a crime.

uphold: Support.

verdict: Judgment or decision.

violate: To fail to follow a law or respect someone's rights.

INDEX

WEBSITES

Due to the changing nature of Internet links, PowerKids Press has developed an online list of websites related to the subject of this book. This site is updated regularly. Please use this link to access the list: www.powerkidslinks.com/courts/federal